KW-053-272

Contents

1.   A Pentecostal Service   5

2.   The Origins of Pentecostalism   11

3.   Three Prominent Personalities   16

4.   Pentecostalism in Britain Today   24

5.   Pentecostal Beliefs   39

6.   The Future   49

Important Dates   52

Further Reading   53

Useful Addresses   54

ACKNOWLEDGEMENTS

Thanks are due to the following, who kindly helped to provide photographs: Pat Thomas and the Fountain Trust (pages 7, 35), Camera Press (page 31), and Luton News (pages 45, 50).

COVER PHOTOGRAPH: *A Pentecostal service. By kind permission of Revd and Mrs Michael Harper.*

The Pentecostal Churches

by

Krister Ottosson

THE RELIGIOUS EDUCATION PRESS
A Division of Pergamon Press

A. Wheaton & Company Limited
A Division of Pergamon Press
Hennock Road, Exeter EX2 8RP

Pergamon Press Ltd
Headington Hill Hall, Oxford OX3 0BW

Pergamon Press Inc.
Maxwell House, Fairview Park, Elmsford, New York 10523

Pergamon of Canada Ltd
75 The East Mall, Toronto, Ontario M8Z 2L9

Pergamon Press (Australia) Pty Ltd
19a Boundary Street, Rushcutters Bay, N.S.W. 2011

Pergamon Press GmbH
6242 Kronberg/Taunus, Pferdstrasse 1,
Frankfurt-am-Main, West Germany

First edition 1977
Reprinted 1978

Printed in Great Britain by A. Wheaton & Co. Ltd., Exeter
ISBN 0 08 021186 0 flexi net
ISBN 0 08 021185 2 flexi non net

1

A
Pentecostal
Service

Dave and Jane first met at the local youth centre. They had been going out together for several weeks, when, one Saturday, Jane said to Dave 'Come to church with me tomorrow'. Dave was reluctant to agree at first but eventually Jane talked him into it.

Next day, they met at the bus station at six o'clock, and walked the half mile to the Elim Pentecostal Church where Jane was a member. Dave remembered thinking that from outside it looked just like the Baptist Church in the road where he lived. As they went through the door, they could hear music coming from inside the building. A middle-aged man greeted Jane, and shook Dave's hand before giving each of them two books. They went through another door and found themselves in the main body of the church. Jane took them to a couple of seats three rows from the back.

Although it was only a quarter past six, there were already about fifty people present, ranging from teenagers to old age pensioners. On the slightly raised platform in front of the large pulpit, eight people were leading the congregation in singing. Of the eight, four were playing guitars, two were shaking tambourines, and two were singing with their hands raised in front of them, moving in time to the music. Dave looked around the church. It was similar to the Baptist church that he knew, with rows of seats facing a high pulpit at the front. The seats were comfortable lift-up cinema seats. He asked Jane why they used that sort of seating. 'Our services are long,' she replied, 'and we shall be here until at least half past eight'.

The sun streamed through the large windows and shone on to the wall behind the pulpit. That wall was decorated with a huge painting of a dove flying downwards towards an open hand. Beside it was an inscription which read, 'I will pour out my spirit upon all flesh'.

For the next quarter of an hour, the group at the front of the church continued to lead the congregation in singing songs from one of the books that they had been given as they came in. It was a book made up of thirty-two duplicated sheets held together by a couple of staples. Jane said that the songs included in the booklet had all been chosen or written by members of the church's youth group. Several of them consisted of passages from the Bible rewritten so as to fit well-known folk tunes.

Just before half past six a young man appeared in the pulpit and stood beside the microphone. He raised his hands, and asked the congregation to stand and sing again a lively chorus that they had just been singing. They stood up, and as the group began to play the introduction, people began clapping their hands, and tapping their feet in time with the music. After the third verse, the minister in the pulpit raised his hand for the congregation to stop singing. He wanted to share with them a few thoughts which had come to his mind while they had been singing that verse. When he had finished speaking, they sang the verse again, and went on to the end of the song. The group continued to play quietly, and the minister whispered several times into the microphone, 'Hallelujah, praise the Lord'. Then he raised his voice and said, 'Let us sing Psalm 150'. Everyone found the psalm in the duplicated booklet, and Dave thought that the original words must have been changed because the version that they sang fitted

A Pentecostal service.

the tune of a current pop song. Half-way through the Psalm, the minister asked if there was anyone in the congregation who had had, during the previous week, an experience for which they wanted to thank God. Three people stood up, one after another – the first, an elderly woman, to say that she had recovered from a bad bout of bronchitis; the second was a man in his early twenties who told how he had been uncertain of what he should be doing with his life: during the week he had asked God for a sign, and he believed that God had replied, and he now felt all his uncertainty had gone. The third person to stand up was a middle-aged woman, to say that her teenage daughter had become a Christian. The singing continued for half an hour, broken by brief sermons from the minister, and contributions from the congregation. One person recited a passage from the Bible; another prayed. During the singing a group of people in the front few rows raised their heads, shut their eyes, and pointed upwards, moving their arms and bodies slowly to the rhythm of the music.

At last the congregation were allowed to sit, the group dispersed, and the minister invited some members of another Pentecostal congregation to take over leading the service for a while. Their minister told how his congregation of about twenty people met in his home for worship every day. Several of them had agreed to share everything that they possessed, just as some of the early Christians had done in the account given in Acts 2:44–45. They spent many hours each week reading the Bible together, and they believed that as they did this, God was leading them to live less imperfect lives. The more they studied the Bible the more they became aware how selfish the values of the world were, and how much Christians were totally dependent upon the inner strength of God to overcome this selfishness.

The visiting minister gave an account of his work, interspersed with invitations to the congregation to sing choruses which emphasised the points he had been making. A member of his congregation told how he had been christened and brought up in a family that never went to church. He had been to Religious Education lessons in school, but it had all seemed like superstition. Then one day, he had been invited to a service in the minister's home, and suddenly the Bible had seemed to come alive: he realised that it was thoroughly relevant to the present day. At that moment he claimed that he had become a Christian.

This section of the service ended with the singing of a hymn from the printed book and then the minister in the pulpit read a passage from the Bible. It was a long passage – the whole of Acts Chapter 2. At the end, he said that he would like to comment on verse 42: 'and they continued steadfastly in the apostles' doctrine and fellowship, and in breaking of bread, and in prayers'. Dave thought it was a long sermon – it lasted more than half an hour. But it was interesting. The preacher spoke with enthusiasm and conviction. He moved around the pulpit when he wanted to emphasise a particular point. He used illustrations to make his sermon clear. He talked a great deal about sin and about the wickedness of the world; and he reminded the congregation that Christians were saved from eternal punishment by the blood of Jesus – the blood which had come from the wounds of Jesus when he was crucified. The minister pointed out that the Apostles' doctrine was another way of speaking about the laws of God, and that these could only be discovered as Christians met regularly together (having 'fellowship') worshipping God in the way that He had laid down (in 'breaking of bread' – the Pentecostal way of describing what other Christian groups call 'services of Holy Communion'), and praying together.

After the sermon, the minister invited any in the congregation who had any problems to meet him after the service. He announced the meetings that were to take place during the week and he reminded people that the following Sunday there was to be a public baptism: three members of the congregation had recently been converted and become Christians, and they wished to be baptised. There was no pool in this particular church so they would hold the service in the local public swimming baths.

The last hymn began, a collection was taken, and then the minister once again whispered several times, 'Hallelujah, praise the Lord'. He announced another chorus, and then another. Twenty minutes later, after several more choruses, the service finally came to an end. It had lasted over two hours. As Jane and Dave went out into the street, his first comment was, 'It didn't seem anything like as long as that'.

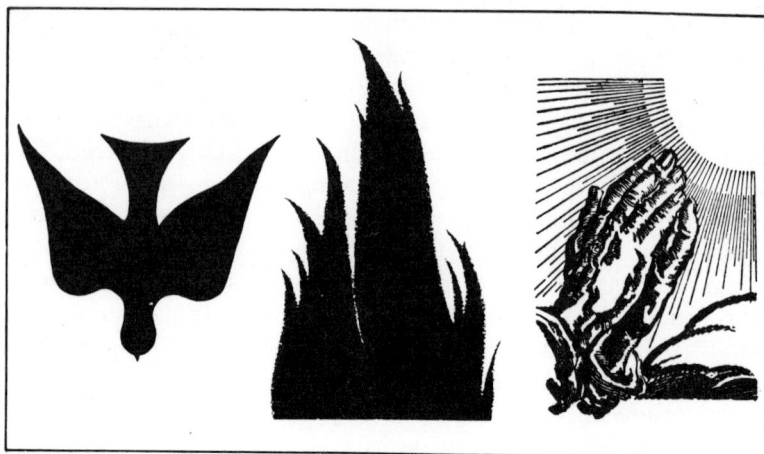

Some typical symbols used by Pentecostal groups.

Think about . . .

Look up Acts 2:44–45. Many people today live together in communities (or communes) sharing some or all of their possessions. Why do you think they do it, and have their reasons always anything to do with those of the earliest Christians?

Find out how different Christian denominations baptise people. Why do you think Pentecostals sometimes use a public swimming pool? Refer to Matthew 3:13–17.

Why do Pentecostals use the symbols shown above, in paintings or on their magazines? (See Mark 1:10–11; Acts 2:3–4; Acts 2:42.)

2

The Origins of Pentecostalism

LOS ANGELES, 1906   Early in 1906, the pastor of the Negro Holiness Church in Los Angeles invited a well-known preacher to speak to the congregation. His name was W. J. Seymour, and he was a pupil of Charles Parham, who led a Bible School at Topeka in the state of Kansas where some wonderful things were said to have happened at religious services: people had been cured of various diseases, alcoholics had ceased to be alcoholics, and non-believers had been converted and become Christians. It was generally thought that God was working miracles in Kansas as a result of the preaching of Parham and his pupils.

Seymour arrived in Los Angeles, and met the pastors and some members of the Holiness Church. The day came for the service, and a large congregation had assembled to hear what Seymour had to say. He stood up to speak, and the people sat back to listen. As he spoke the congregation became more and more serious, and more and more angry at the things he had to say to them. By the time he had finished speaking, the pastor and some of the older members of the congregation had become so angry, that Seymour was put out of the building and thrown into the street.

Why had they become so angry?

Seymour had taken as his text a verse from a section of the Bible which described what happened on the first Whitsunday (the Day of Pentecost), Acts 2:4. 'They were all filled with the Holy Spirit and began to talk in other tongues, as the Spirit gave them power of utterance.' After Jesus had been crucified, some of his followers were meeting together to consider what they should do next. Suddenly, says the book of Acts, a strange thing happened: they all felt a new power, and found themselves speaking in ways that they had never spoken before. All the crowd seemed able to understand them – although they came from many lands and spoke many different languages. The early Christians believed that this event was a sign that the power of God had been given to them to say and do things like those that Jesus had said and done before his crucifixion. When Christians feel within themselves this power to do God's work, the New Testament describes them as 'filled with the Holy Spirit'.

In his sermon to the congregation in Los Angeles, Seymour reminded them of this. But then he went on to tell the congregation that, if they themselves did not have the same experiences as the early Christians, there was something lacking in their faith: they might call themselves Christians, but if they had not had these experiences, the power of God had not *fully* come into them – they were not 'baptised in the Spirit'. It was this that caused some of the congregation to take such offence.

Some members of the congregation, however, were prepared to listen to Seymour, and they invited him to speak at meetings which they held in their own homes.

At one of these meetings, on 9 April 1906, while Seymour was praying aloud, an eight-year-old boy began to speak in a way which no one had ever heard before. He seemed in a highly emotional state, no one understood what he was saying, and he appeared unable to stop himself. Shortly afterwards, the same thing happened to another person at the meeting, and then to another. It was a strange thing to happen, and the only explanation that occurred to the group was that the people concerned had had the same kind of experience as the early Christians on the first Whitsunday. They remembered also that Saint Paul had called this kind of experience 'speaking with tongues' (the new English Bible translates the expression as 'the gift of ecstatic utterance' or 'tongues of ecstasy' – see I Corinthians 12:10, 30). This little group of people took the event as a sign that God was pouring His power into them in a special way, and understood themselves as having been 'baptised in the Holy Spirit'.

Quickly, 'speaking in tongues' spread through the meetings that Seymour held in other homes of members of the congregation of the Holiness Church.

So he hired an old Methodist church building at 312 Azusa Street, and set up his own Mission. More and more people came to this small mission, and more and more people had the experience of being 'baptised in the Holy Spirit'.

From this mission in Azusa Street, Los Angeles, in 1906, the Pentecostal Movement spread throughout the world. There are now more than ten million Pentecostals, and this denomination is at present increasing at a faster rate than any of the other more traditional denominations, particularly in South America. And it all began in the back streets of Los Angeles, in a small, run-down church with sawdust on the floor, and benches made of thick wooden planks laid on empty packing cases.

REVIVAL IN WALES   There had been important religious revivals in Wales in the eighteenth and nineteenth centuries. Pentecostalism in Wales sprang from a later revival.

One day, in 1904, a 'testimony meeting' was under way at a small church in New Quay, on Cardigan Bay. Testimony meetings were religious services at which members of the congregation gave 'testimonies' – told the other members of the congregation what their Christian faith meant to them. There was a long silence – unusually long for services such as this. Suddenly, a woman, Florrie Evans, stood up and said, 'If no one else will, I must say that I do love my Lord Jesus Christ with all my

13

heart'. Immediately, it is said, the rest of the congregation was caught up in a frenzy of excitement. People were weeping and laughing and shouting all at the same time. Then, one person after another stood up and announced that he loved Jesus Christ.

This meeting in 1904 is usually regarded as the beginning of 'the twentieth century Welsh Revival'. For many years, large numbers of Welshmen had become increasingly unsatisfied with the worship in their churches. To their minds it had become too formalised, and appeared to lack enthusiasm. When the Revival began it was as if a new spirit had begun to infect the religious life of Welsh people.

Christians believe in a God who has made himself known in three forms. He is Father, Son and Holy Spirit. When a person hears or reads the story of Jesus (whom Christians call 'the Son of God'), and truly believes it, he is said to put his trust in God through His Son. The test of whether a person's faith is true, some Christians claim, is whether or not that person's life is 'filled with the Holy Spirit'.

The twentieth century Welsh Revivalists felt it important that people should show that they were filled with the Holy Spirit by great bursts of enthusiasm and emotion. It was this outpouring of enthusiasm in religious worship which characterised the Welsh Revival. The traditional sermon became less important, and people took to singing much more than in the past. Congregations would sing for an hour at a time. The prayers would be interrupted frequently, and in the middle of a service an individual member of a congregation would burst into song, and everyone else would join in.

As the Welsh Revival gathered pace, 'speaking in tongues' became a frequent occurrence, and gradually came to be regarded as of more and more importance; it was not sufficient that people should show great emotion when they sang and when they prayed – they had to show also, by uttering strange sounds, that they were 'baptised in the Spirit'. It was this which was later to drive Pentecostalism out of the churches so that it became a new denomination.

But before this happened, the Reverend Alexander Boddy, a

priest in the Church of England, had also come under the influence of the Pentecostal Movement. As a result, the church hall of his Sunderland parish – All Saints – became the first centre in England where people were known to have received 'Baptism in the Spirit' in the way in which the Pentecostalists understood it.

Throughout his life Alexander Boddy remained a priest in the Church of England, thus ensuring that the Pentecostal Movement continued to have a place within the Established Church. But many of those who had experienced 'Baptism in the Spirit' at All Saints, Sunderland, returned home to churches which they felt to be lifeless. As a consequence they set up missions of their own which later became part of a new form of Christianity known as Pentecostalism.

Think about . . .

Alexander Boddy tried to keep Pentecostalism within the Church of England, just as John Wesley (who remained a Church of England minister until he died) tried to do with Methodism. What do you think it was in Methodism and Pentecostalism which forced their adherents to set up new denominations?

Many young people claim that they get bored at church services. Why might they be less bored at Pentecostal services? How important is emotion in religious services?

Try to arrange with a group of friends to attend a service at a Pentecostal church.

3

Three Prominent Personalities

EVAN ROBERTS   Evan Roberts was born in 1888 in Lougher (Glamorgan). He had six brothers and three sisters. His parents were devout Methodists, and the family always went to church and Sunday school together. At the age of 12, Evan became a miner like his father. He was deeply religious, and every free moment he had was spent reading the Bible (even during his lunch breaks down the mines).

In the evenings and at weekends he would watch his friends going out in their boats to fish, and he wanted to go with them. But more than anything else he wanted to feel himself 'taken over by the Spirit of God'. He had made up his mind that he was going to be ready to serve God, and he gave all his attention to preparing himself for that work. He spent hours praying at nights. Most evenings were taken up with some religious activity: on Mondays he would attend a prayer meeting at the Methodist Chapel; on Tuesdays he would attend a prayer meeting for the Sunday School; on Wednesdays he would go to a service at the local church; on Thursdays he attended the meetings of the Band of Hope. It was not surprising that in time he became a great preacher in the mining villages of South Wales. He preached with deep emotion, and the strongest of men could be brought to tears by his oratory.

The life of a coal miner was hard and dangerous. There were many accidents in the pits, and many of the people living in villages made up almost exclusively of coal mining families lived in fear of death or injury. As a result, it was not unusual for some miners, after the last shift had come up on Friday, to spend nearly the whole week's wage packet on drink, in an effort to forget their weariness and fear. Their wives and children suffered because of this, and there was much hardship and unhappiness in many of these mining valleys.

It was to these communities that Evan Roberts went to preach. His preaching changed the lives of many miners and their families. Many of them had used drinking as an emotional escape from reality. Evan Roberts offered them another direction in which they could channel their emotions. Many of them became deeply devout Christians as a result. Instead of going to the pub when they came up from the pits, they would go home, wash, change and go to the village chapels to sing and pray.

Evan Roberts was just one among a large number of preachers, whose work during the Welsh Revival resulted in great changes in the attitudes and lives of working people in parts of South Wales. Drunkenness, gambling, and prostitution all declined in a few years over a large area. This was one of the most spectacular religious events in Britain at the start of the twentieth century.

DONALD GEE   In 1905, in the early days of the Welsh Revival, a fourteen-year-old boy, Donald Gee, was attending a religious service at which the preacher was the famous Methodist evangelist, Seth Joshua. As the preacher moved towards the climax of his address, he reminded his congregation of some passages in the Bible where God was described as being angry with those people who broke His laws. He told the congregation that every one of them was a sinner in the eyes of God, and lived in danger of suffering eternal punishment in the fires of Hell unless he

17

admitted his sinfulness and made up his mind to lead a new and better life. He said that a price (rather like a fine) had to be paid whenever a person committed sin. That price was paid for the whole of mankind when Jesus Christ was crucified. All that was necessary was that people should in their minds picture Jesus on the Cross, say how deeply sorry they were for all the sins that they had committed, claim forgiveness, and set out on a new way of life according to the teachings of Jesus. If they did this, the possibility of eternal life was open to them.

Many members of the congregation were profoundly moved by this appeal, and they came to the front of the meeting to admit publicly that they knew themselves to be sinners, and that from that point onwards they were determined to live life differently. This experience – the feeling of being sinful before God, publicly admitting it, and then being aware of a sense of having been forgiven and of having received a new inner strength to live a better life – is usually called the experience of 'conversion'. When some Christians speak of having been converted on a particular occasion, they are saying that a great change took place in their lives on that day.

One of the people who was converted on listening to Seth Joshua's preaching was Donald Gee. He came forward with the others, and committed himself to a new way of living. For the next seven years he went to religious meetings several times each week.

One day in 1912 he attended the meeting of a Pentecostal congregation. He liked the enthusiastic way in which the people there joined in the singing of the hymns. Everybody seemed happy. During the prayers different people from time to time interrupted by 'speaking in tongues'. He was impressed, and returned again and again. Then one day, all of a sudden, in the middle of the service, he found himself joining in with those who interrupted the speaker; he had begun to 'speak in tongues' himself.

Many years later he was to describe this first experience of 'speaking in tongues' (which Pentecostals call 'Baptism in the Holy Spirit'). 'Increasing glory now flooded my soul as well, until I began to speak in new tongues'. (Quoted from *Pentecost* 1932, p. 9.) He once described what a person felt as he spoke in tongues: 'The soul becomes intoxicated with such a divine ecstasy that it is beyond all ordinary forms of speech' (in an article in the report *Fifth Conference* 1958). 'To see the shining faces of those first praising their Lord in new tongue is to taste something of the very gate of Heaven'. (*Pentecost* 1958, p. 17.)

Donald Gee later became a leader within the Assemblies of God, a branch of the Pentecostal Movement (see Chapter 4). He was pastor of the congregation in Edinburgh for many years and vice-chairman of the British Assemblies of God from 1934 to 1944. In 1947 he became Editor of *Pentecost* which enabled him to influence Pentecostal attitudes throughout the world. In his writings he expressed points of view which were not always shared by fellow Pentecostals. For instance, he had many friends who were not members of Pentecostal churches, and he supported the quest for church unity: he believed that Christians from different denominations and churches should meet with one another in order to learn from one another. From the founding of the World Council of Churches in 1948 Donald Gee tried, in the face of considerable opposition, to build friendly relationships between that body and the Pentecostal movement.

He was involved in disputes with healing evangelists. These were preachers who went to public meetings and offered to heal those who were ill. These evangelists usually claimed that only Christians could be cured in this way. When the cures did not work and people were not healed, the evangelists would claim that the people concerned did not have sufficient Christian faith – there was something lacking in their Christianity. Donald Gee disagreed strongly with this point of view, and frequently wrote articles in which he criticised the healing evangelists for their attitudes.

Another matter over which his views were criticised was his belief that Christians should take part in politics. Within the churches, and particularly within the Pentecostal churches, there have always been large numbers of people that could be called 'Pietists' – people who believe that the world around them is evil, that it cannot be made good, and that therefore Christians must, as far as possible, avoid involvement with those in the world around them. They believe they must study their faith, worship regularly and often with their fellow Christians, and try themselves to lead good lives, but they must not get involved in discussions about politics, let alone become politicians. Donald Gee argued that in order to be a good Christian a person needs to try to make the world a more fair and just place than it is, and there are times when this can only be done through political involvement.

Donald Gee died in 1966 having written two histories of the Pentecostal Movement in Britain – *Glory of the Assemblies of God* and *Story of a Great Revival*. In his lifetime he saw Pentecostalism rise from a spontaneous movement within the traditional churches, break out into a large number of small unrelated congregations, unite to form new groups, and then settle down into distinctive denominations (with all the controversies and arguments that occur in all established Christian denominations) as part of the Christian Church in Britain.

DAVID WILKERSON   David Wilkerson was the minister of a small Pentecostal congregation in Philipsburg, Pennsylvania, U.S.A. On the night of 9 February 1958 he became so bored watching television that he got up, switched the set off, and went into his study. He decided that the two hours that he spent every evening watching television were time wasted, and that he should instead spend those two hours praying. He believes it was that decision which changed the course of his life.

It was during one of these sessions of prayer that he opened a copy of *Life* magazine, and came across an article about a trial currently taking place in New York in which seven boys (all members of a gang which called itself 'The Dragons') were on trial for committing a brutal murder. Suddenly a thought came into his mind: maybe he should go to New York and help those boys. He travelled to New York and went to the trial. He tried to obtain permission to see the boys, but was refused. In desperation he rushed at the judge in open court pleading to be allowed to see the boys in their cells. He was grabbed by two huge American policemen, and thrown out; all the press reporters present photographed the scene and wrote reports of it. Next day all over New York the newspapers carried pictures of a young Pentecostal minister being thrown out of a murder trial by two policemen. The fact that he had been photographed in conflict with the law made him into someone that the New York gangland teenagers felt they could trust. In going around the streets, David Wilkerson came across the brother of one of the convicted murderers. This boy introduced him to members of his own gang, and then later he met other gangs as well. David Wilkerson saw things that horrified him. In *The Cross and the Switchblade* he describes one kind of gang: '. . . the fighting gang, the "bopping" or "jitterbugging" gang. These boys are never far from violence. I know of one instance where a fight took two months to plan; but I know of another case when at two o'clock in the afternoon ten boys were standing around a street corner drinking pop, and at four o'clock that same afternoon one of the boys was dead, two others in the hospital; a major war between rival gangs had flared up, raged and ended in the interval'.

As David Wilkerson came to know some of the members of these gangs, he found that they were all deeply lonely. He discovered that most of them were frightened and insecure, and many were already addicted to drugs. He visited Pentecostal congregations all over the United States, and told them of the things that he had seen in New York. He told them of his scheme to buy a house in the centre of the city and staff it with a group of enthusiastic and caring Christian men and women. He hoped that he could establish a centre which homeless gang members would come to regard as home. He hoped that he and his team of helpers would win the trust and friendship of the members of New York's teenage gangland. And he was doing this because he believed that it was what God wanted him to do.

The congregations listened to what he had to say, they encouraged him, and gave him the money that he needed. In due course a house was bought and staff recruited. It was a dedicated group of people:

'Each morning these young men and women would rise, have breakfast, and then spend the morning in prayer and study. . . . After lunch, our street day would begin. Teams of two or three workers would start walking over a prescribed route, keeping an eye out for signs of trouble. They would be trained to spot the symptoms of narcotics addiction; they would be on the look-out for the teenage alcoholic, or for the girl prostitute. They would talk to gang members, especially the members of fighting gangs. And they would go, not with an eye to gaining converts, but with an eye to meeting need. The conversions would take care of themselves. . . . Most of the teenagers we contacted in this way would not live at the Centre. We would put them in touch with a minister near their home and work through him. . . . But some boys and girls would be sick enough to need special attention. They would be brought to the Centre to live with the community.' (*The Cross and the Switchblade*, p. 118.)

As a result of this work, the lives of many of these young people were totally changed. They stopped fighting in the gang wars. They left the gangs. Some were cured of alcoholism. A few joined the staff of the centre. One went to theological college to train for the ministry. But the most miraculous change of all occurred in a few of the drug addicts. A drug addict who wanted to be cured of his addiction would be brought to the Centre to be 'dried out' – a painful, but occasionally successful, way of breaking an addiction: the person would be placed in a room on his own without access to drugs for three days. During this time he would suffer the agonies of 'withdrawal pains'.

'About two hours after the effect of the final shot wears off, the boy begins withdrawal symptoms. First there is a deep craving which pulls at his body from every pore. Then the boy begins to sweat. He shakes with chills, while his body temperature rises higher and higher. He begins to vomit. He retches for hours on end. His nerves twang with excruciating pain from foot to hair roots. He suffers hallucinations and nightmares more horrible than the worst ever imagined by an alcoholic. This lasts for three full days. And unless he is helped he just won't make it' (p. 149).

Throughout the three days that a person was being 'dried out' the community would make sure that there was someone in the Chapel praying for him. David Wilkerson tells in his book how many young people became Christians. Through meeting members of the staff of the Centre they came to believe in God, and they came also to believe that this God loved them. When they came to this belief they tried to change their lives. Some of them succeeded; others did for a while, and then failed. But for those that succeeded there was a specific point in time when they knew that they had broken with the past. Those who had been drug addicts knew the point at which they had overcome their addiction. It was when they were 'baptised in the Holy Spirit' – 'spoke in tongues' for the first time. That experience, right at the centre of Pentecostal life, was the key experience through which many of those who met David Wilkerson and his colleagues finally conquered the addictions which had previously controlled their lives.

Think about . . .

Think of a number of people who are ill or in trouble of various kinds – for instance those suffering from alcoholism, cancer, pneumonia, heart trouble, a broken leg, or depression. In what ways is it reasonable to expect that some of these people might be helped by prayer and faith? Ask your group leader to arrange a visit by a local Pentecostal minister to talk on this subject and answer questions.

4

Pentecostalism in Britain Today

BACKGROUND Pentecostalism in Britain today is extremely varied: there are small groups meeting in private homes, West Indian groups meeting in rented halls, large groups meeting in buildings that could be mistaken for Methodist churches, and still other groups that go to church in Anglican and Roman Catholic churches on Sundays but meet together for a different kind of worship during the week.

To understand Pentecostals properly you need really to attend their meetings for worship. If one or two groups meet in your area see if you can visit them, perhaps with a friend.

In this section we shall look at the main strands of Pentecostalism that have developed in Britain during the twentieth century. It will be necessary in each case to say something about their historical development.

THE APOSTOLIC CHURCH Christians all agree that what the Bible teaches is true. However, they sometimes disagree over what they think the Bible teaches. For instance, in St John's Gospel 2:1–11, we read of

Jesus at a marriage feast. The story says that when the wine had run out, and Jesus was asked to help, he instructed the servants to fill with water the six large jars used for the Jewish purification rituals. Then he told them to draw some out and take it to the steward in charge of the feast. St John says that when the steward tasted it he found that it had become wine. On reading this passage, some Christians will say, 'This story teaches that Jesus was able to do things contrary to the laws of nature, like changing water into wine.' Other Christians will say, 'It is a mistake to think of this as literally true. For St John it expressed a symbolic meaning – that Jesus had turned the water of Judaism into the wine of Christianity. This Gospel shows the hidden meaning of the life of Jesus. St John calls this "the first of his signs" and goes on to tell of six other "signs" pointing to the significance of Jesus. What John is teaching about Jesus is true – though the stories he uses may not all be literally true.'

For each of these groups of Christians the story is true, but in a different way. These differences of understanding between various Christians concern many sections of the Bible. Those Christians who interpret biblical truth in a generally literal sense represent what is called the conservative evangelical wing of the Church. The Pentecostal group of churches come within this category.

As a result, for example, the Pentecostal churches use New Testament words to describe the tasks undertaken by different people in their congregations, and they also try to recreate in the twentieth century the form of church organisation which the Early Church devised in the first century. The titles that are used for people performing different functions in the congregation include apostles, prophets, shepherds, teachers, evangelists, elders, deacons and deaconesses. The source, for instance, of the use of the word 'shepherd' is I Peter 5:1–5, where the writer describes the Christian community as a group of people that need to be properly cared for, in the same way as a flock of sheep would be cared for by its shepherd. The writer of I Peter was obviously remembering that Jesus spoke of himself as the 'Good Shepherd' (St John's Gospel, Chapter 10).

The first deacons were appointed as described in the New Testament, in Acts 6: the Christian community needed a small number of men to undertake practical tasks like distributing food to the needy. The kind of person who might be appointed to become a deacon is described in I Timothy 3:8–13.

In I Corinthians 12:28, St Paul lists the three main offices in the church in the order that had become accepted in his day: apostles, prophets and teachers. The Pentecostal churches generally use most of these titles.

But, as soon as they did use these words, different Pentecostal congregations understood them in different ways. In the early days of Pentecostalism in Wales, the function of a prophet was understood, apparently, in the way that St Paul intended (see I Corinthians 14:3, 13:2, and 11:4): to give encouragement and comfort to downhearted Christians, and to help other members of the congregation understand what was being said when one member began to speak in tongues. One congregation, at Penygroes near Llanelly in South Wales, did not accept that this was a correct interpretation of the word 'prophet'. The people of that congregation thought that a prophet ought also to be a little like some of the prophets in the Old Testament – he should not only comfort and encourage people: he should also lead the congregation, and speak out against wickedness in the world. In 1918 members of the Burning Bush Assembly in Glasgow found themselves in agreement with the Penygroes congregation. Bit by bit more congregations joined them, and this group of Pentecostal churches became known as the Apostolic Church.

In Britain in 1975 there were 191 congregations of the Apostolic Church, having a total membership of about 4000 people. The Church has a central organisation and administration based at Penygroes: members of individual congregations do not object when they are given instructions from headquarters. The Church publishes a monthly journal, *Herald of Grace*, from its publishing office called the Puritan Press, in Bradford.

Individual members may stand up during services and 'prophesy' on a number of matters: for instance, a person may stand up and condemn drinking; another may stand up and condemn the government's attitude to a war in some part of the world; a third may speak against certain forms of television advertising. Some people get carried away when they prophesy, and it is the task of the most respected members of the Church, the Apostles, to provide balance to the views which members express.

THE ELIM PENTECOSTAL CHURCH   Two brothers, George and Stephen Jeffreys, sons of a Welsh miner, were converted and became Christians during the Welsh Revival. As a result Stephen became an evangelist – a preacher who went around from village to village speaking at religious meetings. He became famous throughout the south of Wales because he was an inspiring preacher, and because he apparently miraculously healed people who were sick. After training for the ministry in the Congregational churches, he set up, in 1915, the Elim Evangelistic Band; this was the team of people that he took with him on his preaching journeys around the country. Wherever this Band went and held meetings, people were converted. If there were sufficient converts in a small area, they formed themselves into a Pentecostal congregation. By 1926 there were so many of these small congregations all over the country that it was decided to set up the Elim Four Square Gospel Alliance. Most of the Elim congregations joined this Alliance. George Jeffreys became its leader. As the movement grew during the nineteen-thirties, a conflict developed: the Jeffreys brothers had always been convinced that people needed to be free if they were to receive inspiration from God; this meant that people should feel free, when they were at religious meetings, to express themselves in any way that they wished – through singing, speaking, clapping or speaking in tongues. They also believed that there should be as little formal organisation within the church as possible. As the denomination grew, it became more and more necessary to create a formal structure within the church. The conflict came to a head in 1939 when George Jeffreys left the Alliance and founded the Bible Pattern Church Fellowship.

A Methodist Chapel in Luton which has become a Pentecostal church.

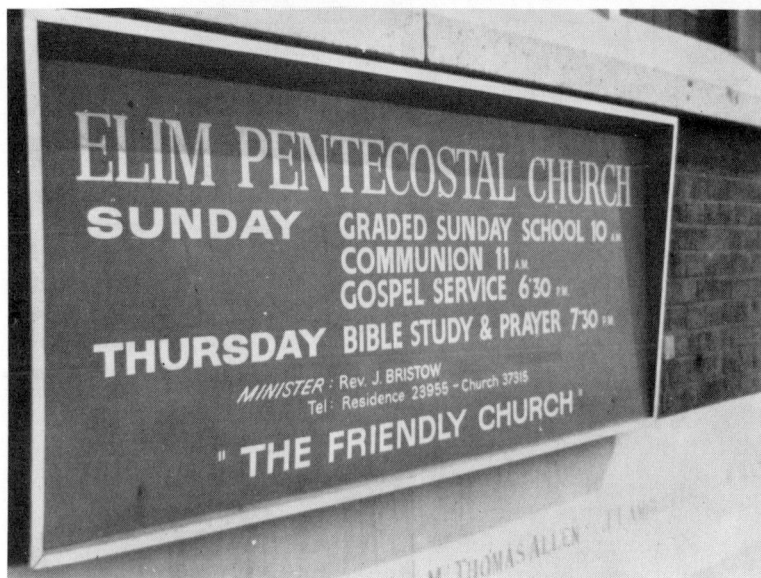

ELIM PENTECOSTAL CHURCH

SUNDAY GRADED SUNDAY SCHOOL 10 A.M.
COMMUNION 11 A.M.
GOSPEL SERVICE 6.30 P.M.

THURSDAY BIBLE STUDY & PRAYER 7.30 P.M.

MINISTER : Rev. J. BRISTOW
Tel : Residence 23955 - Church 37315

" THE FRIENDLY CHURCH "

Originally members of the Elim churches tried to live rigidly according to the Ten Commandments. In addition, for a long time they were not allowed to read magazines, listen to the radio or go to the cinema. Although attitudes have changed in recent years, members of the Elim churches still maintain rigid moral values.

In 1975 the membership of the Elim Pentecostal Church in the United Kingdom was 25 000. There were 310 churches, with 325 ministers, of whom 220 were full-time and paid by the Church.

The Church publishes a journal called the *Elim Evangel*. It also supports its own missionary society (The Elim Missionary Society), which publishes a regular Newsletter providing information about Elim missionaries in Africa, India and South America.

THE ASSEMBLIES OF GOD   The Apostolic Church has a central headquarters in Wales whose authority is respected by individual Apostolic congregations. The Elim Pentecostal Church has a central headquarters in Cheltenham, but this headquarters has only a little authority over individual congregations. The Assemblies of God also have a central headquarters in Nottingham, but it has no authority at all over individual congregations (which in this branch of Pentecostalism are called 'assemblies').

In the early years of the Pentecostal Movement, at the beginning of the twentieth century, there were many, like Alexander Boddy in Sunderland, who saw Pentecostalism as a revival movement within the existing churches – something which would bring new life to what had become dull and boring services. Christians who attended revival meetings frequently discovered a new enthusiasm which they wanted to bring into the life of their congregations at home. In most cases they found that the services to which they returned were too rigid and inflexible to allow for changes, so those who had come under the influence of Pentecostalism would begin meeting separately on weekday evenings while remaining loyal to their churches on Sundays. But it was not long before they began to hire rooms in village halls for meetings on Sundays as well. In this way they slowly broke away from the institutional churches.

On the 1st of February 1924 the Assemblies of God came into being as a nationwide denomination. But the fact that individual local assemblies had grown from existing major denominations made two important contributions to the development of the Assemblies of God.

Firstly, individual assemblies were frequently as different from one another as the major denominations. This meant that it would not have been right to impose a structure upon them. The result is that the Assemblies of God group is the most varied of the larger British Pentecostal churches, and the central head-quarters has no authority at all over individual assemblies.

Secondly, the fact that in the early days members of this branch of Pentecostalism attempted to remain within the churches in which they had grown up indicated that in some cases they liked some of the formal and traditional kinds of worship in those denominations. As a result it is occasionally found that certain Assemblies favour less emotional expression.

In 1975 in Britain there were 541 assemblies with a total membership of around 60 000. There were 416 active ministers, 56 probationary ministers, and 64 retired ministers. In addition there were 54 approved church leaders helping to look after some of the smaller assemblies.

The financial support which Pentecostal Christians give to their churches is considerable. In the Assemblies of God much of this money is used to pay for what they call 'Radio Evangelism' – buying programme time on radio transmitting stations all over the world. They believe that, in this way, instead of a preacher having an audience of fifty or a hundred people in a church, he will have an audience of thousands of people listening in to the radio. Some of these broadcasts can be heard in England. General programme schedules can be obtained from IBRA Radio and those relating especially to the Assemblies of God, from the Assemblies' General Offices (see page 54).

A Healing Service in progress at the Sharon Gospel Church, Manchester (Assemblies of God).

WEST INDIAN PENTECOSTALISM IN ENGLAND   There is a small hall a few miles to the south-east of the centre of Birmingham. During the week it is used for old people's clubs, or other meetings; on Saturdays it is frequently used for jumble sales. But on Sunday mornings and evenings it is used for Christian acts of worship. The noise which comes from this building on these occasions is unbelievable: it seems as if anyone is allowed to take musical instruments into the service with them in order to accompany the singing and the playing. When the people in the hall are not singing or making music it sounds as if they are all shouting 'Praise the Lord' at the top of their voices. This small hall is being used for worship by a West Indian Pentecostal congregation.

There are a large number of West Indian Pentecostal congregations to be found in various parts of Britain. Most of them are affiliated to one of three major churches: the New Testament Church of God, the Church of God of Prophecy, and the Apostolic Church of Jesus Christ. The largest, the New Testament Church of God, came into being in 1953 when a group of West Indian Christians rented premises in the YMCA hall in Wolverhampton. By 1970 the Church was made up of 74

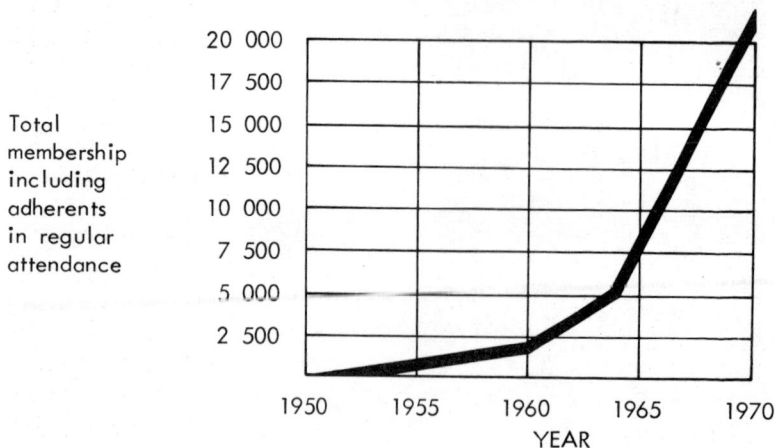

The growth pattern of the New Testament Church of God.
(Source: NTCG, Birmingham)

separate congregations with a combined membership of over 20 000 people. The chart opposite gives an indication of the rate at which this Church's membership has grown.

In the last few years most of the churches in Britain (including the Pentecostal churches) have witnessed a decline in support. In many cases, this decline has been quite dramatic. The New Testament Church of God has been one of the few which has been able to resist this trend – the table below shows that, although the total sect membership has declined slightly, the baptised membership has increased:

	1966	1968	1970	1975
Full-time ministers	15	20	24	85
Baptised membership	2500	3300	3600	4730
Adherents attending regularly	3600	7000	10 000	5500
Sunday school enrolment	4400	5500	7000	10 000
Total membership	10 500	15 800	20 600	20 230

West Indian Pentecostal groups have basically the same beliefs as other Pentecostal groups in Britain: about the Bible, conversion, speaking in tongues, and judgement for sinners. What makes them different is the way in which they worship. Although their services have a pattern, that pattern is flexible, and the individual members of the congregation are encouraged to participate much more than is common among members of white British congregations. The participation takes a variety of forms: one person may stand up and give a 'testimony' (that is, say how and when he became a Christian, and explain the difference that this has made to his life), others accompany the singing with musical instruments, and others call out 'Amen' at various times during the prayers, the sermon or the Bible readings.

There are various reasons given for the rise of West Indian Pentecostalism in Britain. Firstly, for most West Indians, coming to Britain is not only exciting but frightening as well: they come from a warm, pleasant climate where people are relaxed and easy-going, to a chilly, damp climate where people are formal and reserved. So the immigrants feel perplexed and lonely. When, on Sunday, they meet with people like themselves, all their natural happiness and enthusiasm breaks out spontaneously. The only Christian worship which permits the freedom of expression that they need is provided by Pentecostalism.

Secondly, many West Indians who came to Britain tried at first to join English churches. Frequently they encountered either condescension, or, more likely, racial discrimination. So they stopped going to church until they heard of churches made up entirely of fellow West Indians.

Thirdly, between 1955 and 1962, over 260 000 West Indians came to Britain as immigrants. Many of these came believing Britain to be a deeply Christian country. Because they did not understand the way in which Christianity has developed in Britain, many were deeply shocked by the apparent lack of interest in religion, and wrote letters home expressing their sadness. Back home, relatives became concerned and were afraid that some members of their families who had come to Britain might fall away from Christianity and lose their faith. So a small number of West Indian pastors began to leave the West Indies and come to Britain specifically to work in the newly formed churches which were springing up in various parts of the country.

NEO-PENTECOSTALISM On 29 September 1964 a group of people met in a flat in New Cavendish Street, London, above the offices of the Marriage Guidance Council. All those present were Christians who normally attended services in churches of various denominations. However, they had one important thing in common – they had all had religious experiences similar to those which were commonly found in the various Pentecostal churches.

As they talked, they recalled that one of the functions of the Church is to change the world. They realised that institutions which have become dull and uninteresting cannot bring about change. They remembered, from their reading of the New Testament, that the early Christians had seemed joyful, enthusiastic people. What, then, they asked, was lacking in the Christian

A Fountain Trust Festival of Praise in Guildford Cathedral.

churches of the nineteen sixties? What was it that had made them dull and uninteresting? Was it that the churches had become so concerned to structure religious life that it became impossible for anything spontaneous or unusual to happen? Was it that the churches had become too concerned with people having correct beliefs, that they were focusing all their attention on people's minds and not sufficiently on their feelings?

As a result of this meeting, a trust was set up called the Fountain Trust. It is an organisation which hopes for a new religious revival throughout the world, and it believes that this revival can be encouraged through the institutional churches if they will only allow the 'charismatic gifts' to be expressed – 'speaking in tongues' and miraculous healings.

The setting up of the Fountain Trust was a symptom of a

new movement which was developing in strength in the churches at the time. This new movement was Pentecostalism within the mainstream churches – Baptist, Church of England, Congregational, Methodist, Presbyterian, Roman Catholic, Church of Scotland and Church in Wales.

The name by which Pentecostalism in the main institutional churches is known is 'neo-Pentecostalism'.

Since the early nineteen sixties, the movement has grown considerably, and in Britain those congregations which seem best able to resist the trend of declining attendance and membership are those for whom Christianity is more than a formality, and who have allowed their worship to become freer and more spontaneous.

Although, in the early stages, Pentecostalism was rejected by the majority of people within the churches, in recent years neo-Pentecostalism has made some significant advances. In 1974 the Panel on Doctrine of the Church of Scotland published a report (*The Charismatic Movement within the Church of Scotland*) which recognised the presence in the churches of many who wished to encourage the freedom of Pentecostalism. The report recommended that church congregations should not be discouraged from experimentation with Pentecostal-style worship. The most significant advances made by neo-Pentecostalism have been in the Church of England, where whole congregations have taken the decision to regard themselves as Anglican Pentecostals – churches like 'Pip 'n' Jay' (St Philip's and St James') in Bristol and St Hugh's in Luton.

But in the Roman Catholic Church as well there are many Pentecostal groups appearing in various congregations, and they generally have Pentecostal-style acts of worship in people's homes on weekday evenings. It needs always to be remembered that the Pentecostalism of the early years of the twentieth century was intended to be a revival which would change the churches. Very quickly, those who had been affected by it left their churches. It is not possible to tell at the present time whether the same will happen to those who today are finding themselves influenced by neo-Pentecostalism.

THE ECUMENICAL MOVEMENT   One of the most important aspects of church life in the twentieth century has been the desire of the churches to break down the traditional barriers which have grown up between them, and for Christians of all traditions to work more closely together. This is called the 'ecumenical movement'.

One of the results of this movement has been the setting up of organisations which exist to help the churches and missionary societies understand one another better. To British Christians some of the most important of these organisations are the Conference of British Missionary Societies, the British Council of Churches, the Evangelical Alliance, and the World Council of Churches (which has its headquarters in Geneva).

Generally, the Pentecostal churches have opposed ecumenism, and have been extremely critical of the World Council of Churches. Donald Gee was one of the few Pentecostals who wanted to build closer relationships with the W.C.C. But he was frequently criticised for doing so, and one of his great friends, David J. du Plessis, was expelled from the American Assemblies of God for adopting an open-minded attitude to the World Council of Churches.

None of the traditional British Pentecostal churches is a member of the British Council of Churches; but two of them, the Assemblies of God and the Elim Pentecostal Church, are members of the Evangelical Alliance. Some of the African and West Indian Pentecostal churches adopt a more open approach to Christians of other traditions, and have applied for membership of the British and World Councils of Churches.

The Pentecostal churches are generally hostile towards the Roman Catholic and the Eastern Orthodox Churches.

Think about . . .

You can get a good idea of the character of the various Pentecostal groups by reading their magazines and newspapers. Churches receive many requests for copies of their publications, and are usually happy to oblige; however, meeting all these requests can be very expensive, and they appreciate it if enquirers enclose a stamped addressed envelope and make a contribution towards the cost of the materials requested. Send for copies of the following magazines (addresses of headquarters may be found on page 54).

Herald of Grace (10p) – the official magazine of the Apostolic Church – from The Puritan Press Ltd.

World Pentecost (25p) – the official magazine of the Pentecostal movements of the world.

Redemption Tidings (10p) – the official magazine of the Assemblies of God.

Renewal (annual subscription £1.75) – the bimonthly magazine of the Fountain Trust.

There are also radio programmes organised by the Pentecostal movement, broadcast on Radio Trans-Europe, Lisbon, on 31.02m short wave. Programmmes in English are broadcast on Fridays at 20.45 G.M.T., Saturdays at 20.30 G.M.T., and Sundays at 20.30 G.M.T. Try to listen in to some of these programmes.

5

Pentecostal Beliefs

THE BIBLE   When a member of a Pentecostal Church is asked what is the significance of the Bible in his religion, he would probably answer by saying something like, 'The Bible is the inspired Word of God'. By this he means a number of things:

1.   The Bible is true in a literal sense: If the Bible says that the world was created in six days, then that is what Pentecostal Christians will generally believe, irrespective of what scientists or anyone else may say.

2.   The Bible is the Christian's authority on ethical matters. If a Christian is unsure how he should act in a particular situation, he should be able to find out from the Bible how to distinguish right from wrong in those circumstances. Some Pentecostals have become conscientious objectors to military service because of the commandment 'Thou shalt not kill'.

3.   The Bible provides the basis for every sermon. In some British churches today it is possible to hear sermons in which there is no explicit reference to any passage or verse from the Bible. Such a thing could not happen in a Pentecostal church. The Pentecostal preacher is expected to begin his sermon with a verse

from the Bible, and then try to explain its meaning by relating it to other passages. Throughout his sermon he uses biblical phrases which have become part of his normal vocabulary.

4.   The Bible provides the basis for the individual's devotional life. Many Pentecostals read a short passage from the Bible each day, and then spend some time thinking about it and trying to apply what they have read to their everyday lives. For instance, on reading the passage in the New Testament in which Peter asked Jesus how often he should forgive those who had wronged him, and received the answer that for the Christian it was never possible to stop forgiving, a devout Pentecostal would spend time thinking about all the people who had wronged him by hurting him or treating him unfairly. He might then pray for God's help to be less resentful of all these people.

5.   The Bible provides the pattern for Christian living today. Pentecostals believe that things happened in New Testament times precisely as the Bible tells us they did, and also that Jesus established a pattern for Christian living. Therefore they believe that Christians today are expected to do many of the things that Jesus and the first disciples were able to do. Thus Pentecostals believe in trying to perform healing miracles.

It is important to realise, however, that there is frequent disagreement between Pentecostals (even within the same church) about attitudes to the Bible. While what has been said above is generally true for most Pentecostal Christians, it is possible to find some who have different points of view.

BEING SAVED   Most Pentecostals believe in what is generally called the 'three stage way of salvation'. They believe that a person is saved in the moment that he is converted (see the section on Donald Gee), that after conversion he needs to be baptised by total immersion in water; and that at some later stage he may receive the baptism of the Holy Spirit and begin to speak in other tongues. (See Acts 2:4, 10:46, 9:17, 19:6.)

Pentecostals believe that 'the baptism of the Holy Spirit' is available to all true Christians if only they will allow themselves

A Pentecostal Church in Watford.

Jesus said:
"I AM THE RESURRECTION AND THE LIFE: HE THAT BELIEVETH ON ME, THOUGH HE WERE DEAD, YET SHALL HE LIVE"
John 11.25

to become aware of it. They believe that many Christians consciously or unconsciously close themselves to the possibility of receiving 'the baptism of the Holy Spirit', and that this closing of themselves against a gift from God is a great sin.

Why do people need to be saved? And from what do people need saving? Pentecostal Christians believe that human beings are basically evil. They believe that even the apparently good deeds of people are motivated by selfish interests. They believe that originally, when God created the Universe, God created man perfect. But when tempted he succumbed, and 'fell from grace'. (Read the story in Genesis 3.) From that point, each succeeding generation of human beings inherited Adam's sinfulness.

Pentecostals believe that man's sinfulness is so great that only God can save him from the punishment which he deserves. They teach that all sin and evil demands a price which has to be paid – like a prison sentence or a fine which a convicted criminal is obliged to pay. But they hold that the price to be paid for man's rebellion against God is so great that no man can ever pay it in full.

But God himself can pay the fine. Pentecostals teach that in fact He did this once and for all for everybody when he sent His son, Jesus Christ, into the world. The price was finally paid when Jesus was crucified. In this act of sacrificing His Son, God paid all that ever needed to be paid for man's sinfulness. This is why Pentecostals speak so often of the 'blood of Jesus'. Once a person has realised the seriousness of his sin, believes that Jesus really is the Son of God, and is converted, he is a bit like a criminal accepting the fact that someone else has served his sentence for him.

Once a person is 'saved' he is expected to spend the rest of his life trying to learn more about the will of God for mankind. This involves becoming a member of the Church, and sharing in its activities. As Christians grow in their spiritual life, they are said to be ready to 'inherit eternal life' – to live eternally in God's presence.

Many Christians are unhappy about the Pentecostal emphasis

on the sinfulness and wickedness of human beings. They believe that this attitude is based on a literal understanding of a story (the story of Adam and Eve) that was originally probably little more than a myth, a story told to illustrate truth and make it easier to understand. They would go on to point to the large number of passages in the Gospels of Matthew, Mark, Luke and John in which God is described as good, loving, caring and forgiving, and passages in which Jesus helped, healed, comforted, encouraged and forgave people that he met, irrespective of their beliefs or the number of times they went to the Temple or the Synagogue.

LIFE AFTER DEATH   In their magazine, *Redemption Tidings*, the Assemblies of God state their beliefs which include the following: 'We believe . . . in His (Jesus Christ's) pre-Millenial Second Advent; . . . in the Everlasting conscious Bliss of all Believers, and the Everlasting Conscious Punishment of all those whose names are not written in the Book of Life'. These beliefs are based on passages in the Revelation of John (the last book in the Bible). The visionary language of John is taken literally and concretely. This means that Pentecostals expect Jesus Christ to return physically to earth, and those who have died as Christians will be raised to experience everlasting happiness. He will rule the world for a thousand years before the final Day of Judgement. On that final Day, they believe, there will be a general resurrection (all those who have ever lived and died, will be raised from the dead), and those who rejected Christ will begin their everlasting punishment.

Pentecostals are not the only Christians who have these beliefs about life after death. They share these beliefs with many other Christians belonging to the conservative evangelical wing of the Churches.

Many Christians who do *not* share this point of view claim that these beliefs turn Christianity into a religion of fear; they cannot believe that a God of love would try to win people over to Him by the use of fear. They also say that the Revelation of St John was written in a time when Christians were being persecuted under the Roman Empire, and were expecting Jesus to return to earth to rule the world. Like many other parts of the Bible, it is to be understood allegorically and not literally. For example, when a boy says a particular girl is the most wonderful girl in the world, he is speaking allegorically: he is saying something about his feelings towards her (and therefore is expressing a kind of truth), but he is not claiming to have studied every girl in the world and can prove that what he says is literally true.

RIGHT AND WRONG In the early days of the growth of the Pentecostal churches, they adopted a very strict code of ethics. Smoking and drinking were not allowed, neither was the wearing of make-up, nor activities like dancing and theatre-going. Later, Pentecostal Christians were discouraged from going to the cinema, and women from wearing mini-skirts and short hair. Sunday has always been regarded as a day of rest to be observed with strictness – it has always been the rule that no unnecessary activity should be undertaken on that day.

During a period of history when there were many in society who upheld strict codes of ethical behaviour, Pentecostals were some of the most strict. However, in the last ten years there have been considerable changes in society's attitudes, and the attitudes of Pentecostals have been modified too, though they still remain strict by comparison with those of most other Christians.

Among Christians today, Pentecostals have some of the strictest standards on matters like sexual ethics, marriage and divorce, swearing, abortion, and personal honesty. Pentecostals tend to be extremely law-abiding citizens, and would not support acts of civil disobedience even though such acts may be intended to draw attention to unjust laws or the plight of the needy.

Members of Pentecostal churches try to 'tithe' – i.e. give one tenth of their income to the church. The high level of weekly giving by members of the Pentecostal churches explains how it is that these churches can support a substantial number of missionaries in schools, hospitals and missions in many parts of India, Africa, and South America.

MIRACLES AND HEALING In the early days of the Pentecostal revival, at the beginning of the twentieth century, there were some preachers who were known as healing evangelists. They preached to great audiences and congregations, and asked that those who had any illness from which they wished to be cured be brought forward at the end of the meeting. They would then place their hands on the heads of the people who came forward, and pray that they might be cured. Some of the illnesses would be physical (like broken arms, or sprained wrists, or tuberculosis), some would be clearly emotional or psychological (like drunkenness), and some would appear to be physical but have psychological causes (like some kinds of back-ache). It seems clear from the accounts of some of these meetings that many people were 'cured', but because of the emotion surrounding the events, and

MIRACLE HEALING

Elderly man is cured of cancer

A LUTON vicar claims cancer and brain damage are being cured miraculously in his parish.

According to the Reverend Colin Urquhart, vicar of St Hugh's, Lewsey, prayer has cured an elderly man, seriously ill with cancer, and a two-year-old "human vegetable."

The practice at the church was first reported over three years ago in the Luton News.

The "miracles" are told in a recent book, When the Spirit Comes, about Mr Urquhart's ministry in Luton. Published only in December, thousands of copies have already been sold.

Mr Urquhart, who is married with three children, said: "The Christians here know God as a real person, and their lives are filled with his power.

"That is why miracles are happening here, and healing is just one of those miracles."

Spiritual healing has been practised at St Hugh's for some years now. In December, 1971, the Luton News reported a meeting between senior church leaders on the practice at the church.

"I have known hundreds of people who needed help," said Mr Urquhart. "Some are healed quickly, others

---

By SUE HICKENBOTTOM and ANDREW RILEY

---

need regular help over a period of months. All have been greatly blessed. People should not come to me with thanks, but should praise God."

In his book, Mr Urquhart, who has been vicar of St Hugh's for the past five years, reveals several occasions when illnesses have been cured following prayer sessions.

He cites the cases of many people, including a young boy with bronchitis, cured without hospital treatment. He maintains that these are just instances of God renewing the Church.

The activities at St Hugh's have been given the full support of higher members of the Church hierarchy.

The Right Reverend John Hare, Bishop of Bedford, commented this week: "I believe in divine healing, and practise it myself. I have never yet known anything but good to come of it."

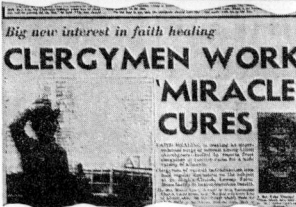

Big new interest in faith healing

CLERGYMEN WORK 'MIRACLE' CURES

Flashback to Luton News story in December 1971

45

the exaggerated ways in which they were reported, it is difficult to be sure about the kinds of cures effected.

Many of the early healing evangelists preached that people could be cured of any sickness they might have, if only they had sufficient faith, and that if they were not cured, this was a sign that their faith was inadequate. In the main Pentecostal churches in Britain, there has been a gradual move away from a belief that physical disease can be cured solely by prayer. It is still, however, recognised that some kinds of illness can be, and frequently are, cured as a result of an experience of conversion (see the section on David Wilkerson). In Britain, those churches in which a majority of members still believe that miracles (understood as a direct interference with the physical laws of nature) do happen are to be found among the newer African and West Indian Pentecostal congregations. As well as in these churches in Britain, the miraculous healing side of Pentecostalism is held to be of considerable importance in Pentecostal churches in Africa and South America.

DEMONS Pentecostals believe that the Devil is a real being, and that he is constantly at war with God. They believe that it was the Devil that caused Adam and Eve to sin by eating the forbidden fruit in the Garden of Eden. They believe also that every temptation that comes to the Christian is a temptation from the Devil which the Christian must resist.

Pentecostals also believe that people can have their personalities taken over by devils – they can become 'possessed'. Pentecostals will frequently say that (for instance) alcoholics, inveterate gamblers, people addicted to drugs, and people with fiery tempers are possessed of devils of drink, of gambling, of drugs, and of temper respectively. They believe that it is possible to 'cast out' (or exorcise) some of these devils.

Generally speaking, Pentecostals treat a person whom they regard as possessed of a demon in the same way as they treat a person who is not a Christian – they pray that the Spirit of God will 'take over' that person and drive out the demon and the lack of faith. In other words, they pray that God will cast out the demon. On the whole they do not practise exorcism (i.e. try to drive out the devil themselves).

In recent years in Britain there has been an increasing interest in demonology and exorcism. There are generally two groups of people who involve themselves in this: on the one hand there are those who have little or no contact with the churches. It is sometimes said of such groups that they are frequently practising witchcraft. On the other hand there are Christians who have come into contact with Pentecostal and neo-Pentecostal groups, and believe that the ability to cast out demons is one of the powers given to Christians when they are 'baptised in the Holy Spirit'. Those in the churches who disapprove of exorcism and belief in demons argue that it is better to send a sick person to a doctor or a psychiatrist, than to an exorcist.

INTERPRETATION   In I Corinthians 14 Saint Paul devotes a large section of his letter to speaking in tongues. The main point that he makes is that ecstatic speech is only of benefit to the speaker himself. He insisted that when Christians met together for worship they should try to be of help to one another – to assist one another in learning more about God. Speaking in tongues would only help all the members of the community if someone was able to interpret what was being said – it might be the speaker himself, or it could be someone else. Therefore Paul suggested that three people speaking in tongues in one meeting was quite sufficient – if someone was to come into the meeting room who didn't understand what was happening, he might think that the Christian community was mad (I Corinthians 14:23).

Think about . . .

Most Christians believe the statement 'The Bible is true'. But different Christians have different ideas of what this means. Look at the following passages in the Bible and discuss some of the different ways in which different Christians will regard them as true:

> Genesis 1; Genesis 3; Luke 15:11–32; John 11:38–44; Revelation 20:11 to 21:4.

Many people are attracted to various religious groups because they seem lively and interesting. How important is it to consider also the things they believe?

Consider some of the arguments for and against Christians breaking the law when they think that a particular law is wrong.

6

The
Future

Some people think that there are two major criticisms that can be made of the traditional churches in Britain today. The first is that they have become 'institutionalised' – they have developed a pattern into which newcomers have to fit. The language that they use is the language of previous ages; the attitudes that they adopt are the attitudes of earlier generations; their services have become ritualised formalities. It is difficult for them to change, and if change does come, it comes very slowly.

The second major criticism is that they place more emphasis on people's minds than they do on their feelings – the churches' worship has been developed into 'correct' forms and patterns, but these do not express the real feelings and emotions of most people today.

Pentecostalism tries to say: 'Get rid of your rituals and your institutions, and let people be free to express their deepest religious feelings.' It goes on to say that Christianity is not only for people who are brainy and who can talk theology – Christianity is for everyone.

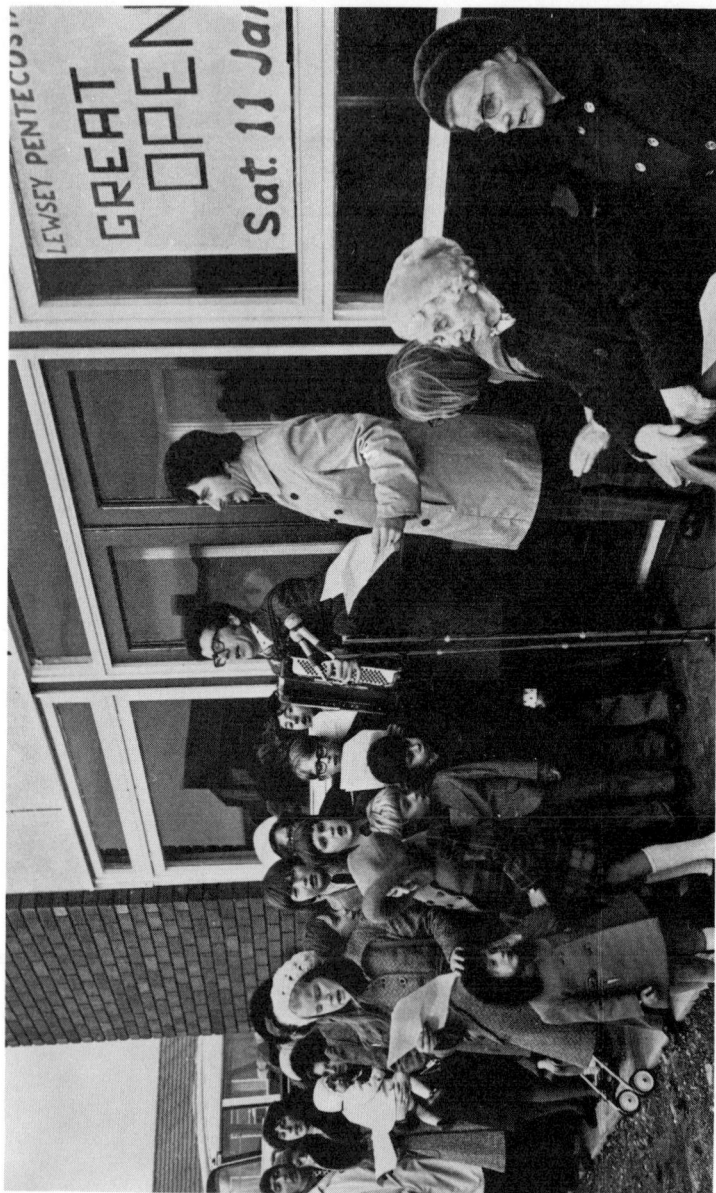

The opening of a Pentecostal Church in Luton.

There are signs today that the traditional churches are beginning to take Pentecostalism seriously. But there is a considerable amount of suspicion on all sides: on the whole the Pentecostal churches are afraid that if they get too close to the traditional churches, they themselves will become 'institutionalised' (some of their critics argue that this has already happened to them). They also fear that their own fundamental beliefs will be compromised and watered down, particularly their insistence on the importance of 'baptism in the Holy Spirit'. Many in the churches are suspicious of what they regard as the 'magical' elements in Pentecostalism – they would like more rational and scientific analysis to be made of things like 'speaking in tongues' and 'miraculous' healings.

The danger is always that any new movement in the churches will end up by dividing the churches and creating more splinter groups and denominations. It is difficult to see how this can be avoided when many of these groups try to claim that they alone are right and that all the others are wrong. This has tended to happen throughout church history. Only recently have the churches begun to realise that no single denomination can be right on every matter. It is only in the twentieth century that Christians have begun to realise that each can learn from the other's point of view.

For this reason it would seem important that Pentecostals should try to share their beliefs and insights with other Christians, and in their turn learn from some of the insights of the other churches. This will always be difficult, but it is something that Christians must always try to do.

Think about . . .

What are some of the lessons that the traditional churches can learn from Pentecostalism?

What are some of the things that Pentecostalism can learn from the traditional churches?

Important Dates

1904   Beginning of the Welsh Revival.

1906   9th April: The 'fire comes down' at a prayer meeting in Bonnie Brae Street, Los Angeles – the beginning of present-day Pentecostalism.

1907   Alexander Boddy is drawn into Pentecostalism – Pentecostalism comes to England.

1908   Revival spreads to Scotland (Kilsyth).

1909   Formation of the Pentecostal Missionary Union.

1915   Formation of the Elim Evangelistic Band.

1924   Pentecostal Missionary Union dissolved and replaced by The Assemblies of God.

1926   Elim Four Square Gospel Alliance formed.

1939   First World Pentecostal Conference (Stockholm).

1953   New Testament Church of God comes into being.

1964   Founding of the Fountain Trust.

1974   The Church of Scotland gives qualified approval to neo-Pentecostalism.

Further Reading

Black Churches – West Indian and African Sects in Britain by CLIFFORD HILL (British Council of Churches, 1971).

The Pentecostals by WALTER J. HOLLENWEGER (SCM Press, 1972).

Ecstatic Religion by I. H. LEWIS (Penguin Books, 1971).

They Speak with Other Tongues by JOHN L. SHERRILL (Hodder and Stoughton, 1965).

Can the Pentecostal movement renew the Churches? by EMMANUEL SULLIVAN, SA (British Council of Churches, 1972).

Useful Addresses

The Apostolic Church
General Headquarters, Penygroes, Llanelly, Carmarthen, South Wales.
Missionary Office, Great Horton Road, Bradford 7, Yorkshire.
Publishing Office, The Puritan Press, 353 Great Horton Road, Bradford 7, Yorkshire.

Assemblies of God in Great Britain and Ireland
General Headquarters, Editorial and Publishing Office, 106–114, Talbot Street, Nottingham NG1 5GH.

Elim Pentecostal Church
General Headquarters and Missionary Society, St George's Road, Cheltenham, Gloucestershire.

New Testament Church of God
Registered Office, George Street, Lozells, Birmingham B19 1ND.

The British Council of Churches, 10 Eaton Gate, London SW1W 9BT.

The Evangelical Alliance, 19 Draycott Place, London SW3 2SJ.

The Fountain Trust, 3a High Street, Esher, Surrey.

IBRA Radio, Pentecostal Church, Roise Street, Bedford.

World Pentecost Magazine (a quarterly review of world-wide Pentecostal activities, published at the request of the World Conference of Pentecostal Churches), The City Temple, Cowbridge Road, Cardiff, Wales.